A Snake Charmer's Assistant

Sophie Norton

ISBN: 9798487877031

Cerasus Poetry
London N22 6LY

cerasuspoetry.com

'All was quiet in the deep dark wood.
The mouse found a nut and the nut was good.'

- Julia Donaldson

Contents

Accidents Happen

I've written a book
but my mum won't let me
drive on the motorway.
I'm writing on the
motorway when I tell her:
"Guess what Mum,
I've written a book!"
She swerves. "Don't
go driving on the
motorway, you might
accidentally write
another one. It's always
the same. People don't
set out to have
accidents or to write
books but motorways
are funny places.
Very unpredictable."

A Patient Affair

My therapist knows all about you.
What makes you tick in Times New Roman.
She's concerned about your alcohol intake
and the way you brush your hair.
During my previous appointment she was acting
rather questionably. Didn't prop the door open
and sported three different shades of nail polish
on her thumb alone. She talked me into developing
diabetes and when I declined she started screaming
like a diseased elephant or a smoked-out husk.
On the bus home I kept thinking about
all the secrets I'd told her; your favourite fruit
and the way you burp in your sleep. I was avoiding
eye contact with the driver when the man
in the seat next to me started gesticulating in Spanish.
He mistook me for his brother-in-law so I followed him home
and was just beginning to assist with filing his tax reports when
it occurred to me that the situation was suspicious.
I interrogated him about ulterior motives but his answers
seemed perfectly satisfactory.
He provided me with tea for my trouble and I stayed there
until he threw a fig cake at my head like a hockey puck
and I thought the day had been bizarre enough already.

27 Volts

I'm on my way to Lithuania tomorrow,
when the freedom fighters fall
and the cake decorators seize the city.
I expect tangy lime and cerulean zizzle
but the most unexpected arrival
will surely be the battery-acid concoction
in a shade of lemonade yellow.
It's the secret component of the electric
covid-19-free meringues
that the decorators are most liable for.
A tax collector approached me
in a satellite-plated van and
announced his departure from God.
He had baskets upon baskets of fruit.

Rules and Regulations

A man sits by a fountain
and contemplates his existence
when the fountain becomes a goldfish
and he becomes the tank.
He may be unaware of the requirements,
however each marine habitat
must be at least 3.5 times
the volume of its occupant.
Failure to comply
may result in solitary confinement.
Take me to a museum and
I'll have a religious experience
among the skeletons and the dust.
Is it appropriate to wear a dead man's
suit to his funeral? Close the pearly gates,
shut down the party and bring out the encore.
This dichotomic state of affairs has lost its sting.

Operation X

There's an uneducated man
with an unsterilised knife
rummaging through my spleen!
I told him I didn't think
the operation was strictly necessary
and he would have let me go if it wasn't
for the fact that I disagreed vehemently
with his concept of fashion.
He wore loafers instead of sandals,
and a suit jacket hung on the wall
in place of a qualification.
Oh Lord the infested scalpel
has reached my trachea
and my teeth are coppery.
Hold off the alveoli!! Save the bronchi
and sponsor a seal in the south of France.
There's a street somewhere
lined with the slippers of all the Cinderellas
who didn't need a prince to solve their problems.
The Big Issue has replaced Kleenex tissues
and the news agencies are crying with jealousy.
My surgeon has finished and he wipes
my pleural fluid on his shirt lapel with efficiency.
The intersectional webs between my ribs
have torn and I hang my head in shame.

Belinda

I once had a twin called Belinda, who lived in the kitchen cupboard until we were eight. Soon after emerging she developed schizophrenia and died from a frying pan to the head. Later that summer I gave birth to myself on a McDonald's restroom floor, nail scraping sentences in the grime and piss.

A Christian skinhead told me never to believe my mother and I said "don't worry, she just pretends to be me". We're both narcissistic to the core but I'm the better liar. When Belinda finally returned, I took her life in a spiralizer, hips gyrating to the beat. The TV producers shoved napalm in my drawers but they forgot to bring the gasoline.

Talent tastes like a tight-fitting, neoprene, Santa-Monica club scene where everyone has tongues for arms and the light bulbs don't stop spitting. I shaved my head above an ergonomic freeway and deny the claims that it was staged. I don't think my achievements have ever rivalled the effectiveness of my birth, a comedic strategy where nobody was amused.

Consumer Culture

My melatonin left me for another man,
looked me dead in the eye with a smile.
This life is made of metaphors,
most of them still waiting to happen.
We're hypocrites of unethical consumerism
with our alien imports and subterranean meals.
Gluttonous pigs held in a refractory watering can.
The big man raises his fist and we all start laughing.
Your frilly socks aren't welcome here.
When I describe this age to my daughter
I'll use terms such as "ergonomic" and "contraband".
A catfish lures the fishmonger on
but the police don't bother to enforce that sort of thing.
She'll have to fend for herself,
rubber gloves in a packet of crisps.
A motorway pile-up in the present tense,
she's got quite the job on her hands.

Lashing Out

I'm lurking by the edge of a lake in Stavanger
when a man approaches me from behind.
He crunches a twig with the whip crack
of a smack den and everything turns blue.
Picture a freeze-frame in the back of space,
we're floating upwards on the bottom of the lake
and my mullet is caught in the reeds.
I discover that my companion's name is Larry,
and I make sure not to question him
about his manifestations, as I'm certain he's a
secretive man. I'm banging my head
on the side of the lake and I hear
the stingrays spilling my secrets again
but I can't do anything to shut them up.
More shots to come -
two buffoons on a bicycle come careering
through my thoughts, smashing road signs
on their way to the village fair.
There's a merry-go-round of laughter
but the candy floss tastes sour.
I feel a tugging on my left foot and
Larry has disappeared!
He definitely died, I'm certain of this
but I suppose dead weights are easier to conceal.
My brain is screaming, "I'm sick of this lake! Take me
back to Puerto Rico where my soul may wave
manically at the mysterious Marines in the bay."

Coronary Heart Disease

Have you ever come
home for the weekend
and seen your father
slumped on the settee
swollen as a toenail? A
chortled chorizo in a
wedding gown two sizes
too small, stuffed-up budgie
on a sausage roll platter.

Spending the Afternoon in Sudan

I got a piercing in a pandemic
just to get the ball rolling. A clean
sweep off the back of my feet,
I found myself in a laundromat.
There was no air conditioning,
and the drums were full of hand
sanitiser. Fast forward half an hour,
I'm falling out a window with a
wrist braced against the carpet.
The authorities were called
but there was no sign of a break-in
so they packed up and buggered off.
I'm lying there with a broken head
in a puddle of my own despair,
cursing the judicial system. Enter Lucifer.
He slouches like there's something wrong
and begrudgingly takes my order.
We're sharing fizzy drinks and a portion
of chips and before I know it I'm back
on my feet. A flash flood destroyed
my jeans as I was about to leave
but luckily we were still in the laundromat.
A few tabs of breezy lavender and
I'll be on my way.

Pando

A depressed man turns on the tap to dilute
some bleach. He's decided to die in his best suit
but forgets to empty the sink full of fruit
that he picked from his garden straight from the root.
He's a considerate man so he uses a silencer to mute
the bang and prepares to shoot.

Before the man gets chance to shoot
he remembers the bleach that he forgot to dilute.
'What a way to die' he thinks then decides to mute
that thought and puts the gun back in his suit.
He can't decide how to die so his feet root
themselves to the floor and he turns to the fruit.

He thinks its a waste not to eat the fruit
because nobody will eat it after the shoot,
so he takes a swig from his root
beer bottle then uses the tap to dilute
that too because the taste doesn't suit
him. He forgot to take the TV off mute

which was silly because he needs something to mute
the doubt in his mind while he eats his fruit.
He bites into a strawberry but it doesn't suit
the root beer taste and now he's not sure if he should shoot
when the last thing he'll ever eat is a dilute
drink and a fruit. The TV talks about the oldest tree root

which is 80,000 years old. The man isn't interested in an old root
so once again the TV sound is turned to mute.
The bad tasting strawberry has helped him dilute
his thoughts and now he's hungry for more fruit.
He thinks, 'I don't have time to pick fruit and shoot!'
and in his distraction he spills beer on his suit.

Now he's livid because he doesn't have another suit
to die in but there's a stain and everyone will know about the root
beer. He's so angry that he no longer wants to shoot
himself but instead the suit and in a mute
rage he fires his gun at the fruit.
He misses and hits the bleach which he forgot to dilute.

The bottle bursts from the shoot and expels bleach onto his suit
which he DID NOT DILUTE but the bullet ricochets itself into the root
on the mute screen. Sparks! And the dead man slumps onto his fruit.

Insider Intel

I've been informed that the inhabitants of Heaven have access to unlimited toilet roll. They dine on Oreos and wine for lunch (except every other Tuesday, when they enjoy a spit roast instead). I wonder if they ever combine the two and spit in their wine, or roast their Oreos. Maybe they get drunk off the wine and start wrapping themselves in toilet rolls like Egyptian corpses and pretend they're rotting in the afterlife. Or maybe, because there are unlimited rolls they strap them to their backs and pretend they're space explorers, discovering the stars for the first time.

Perhaps they fuel the spit roast fire with the cardboard centres from the toilet rolls. Or maybe the cardboard is used to build little cardboard villages full of little cardboard people who don't know any better. What if the inhabitants wrapped themselves in cardboard and drank enough spit roast to set the toilet roll on fire? Is the toilet roll really unlimited? Does anyone bother to raise a glass of wine to the unlimited toilet roll and the roasted pigs that they shamelessly enjoy every other Tuesday? The wine is best served at room temperature. I hope the fire isn't too hot.

I AM

My mother's financial issues.

The moth on my bedside light.

Keeping quiet about the Romans.

A crash test collision course.

An advocate for loose ends.

A martini made with Vermouth.

Reluctantly German.

A teenage trip to Disney World.

Michelangelo's test run.

Perpetually unimpressed.

The Christmas decorations packed away in the loft.

A professional figure skater.

My uncle's grey tooth.

Giggling at the back of my wardrobe.

A broken toenail.

Lingering snot.

The instrument used to defrost a small portion of peas.

A snake charmer's assistant.

Dementia's worst nightmare.

Toxic masculinity.

An atomic bomb.

A danger to insurance companies everywhere.

America's sweetheart.

Shakespeare with a sobriety complex.

Feeling anxious.

A mouthful of tubes.

Taking too long on the toilet.

A thoroughbred racehorse.

Shouting in cursive.

Fantastic gums.

Neglecting responsibilities.

Battling a brain tumour.

Sorting my affairs.

Growing increasingly uncomfortable.

Fluent in Norwegian

A raging pitbull.

Sordidly obese.

Available for commission.

Enjoying this.

Murder on the Dancefloor

you released my hand
and I collapsed like a sack.
deflated lung popped balloon
at a children's birthday party.

a fish escapes from his tank but
suffocates himself in the process.
pressing air through double glazing,
his slimy spasms recede damp.

There's a welcome release of tears
"Congratulations", the floodgates are open
and ready for business. What a sorry state,
you should have seen this coming.

Communist Rant

Fuck the man in the ugly suede jumper!
There's a political party in progress
and all he does is shake people's hands.
Is he not aware that he's licking the
equivalent of 45 door knobs per minute
with the battery power of a pontooning
pig pumped full of steroids? He's the
downfall of us all, the rabbit's trap! He
splits his sequences with unparalleled
precision, a surgeon in a suit-and-tie.

He's buffering the scales, would do
anything to retain that small portion of
power. Life in the control room must be
half cramped but there's a refusal to be
candid. Lights are up, cameras are ready
and refreshments are only a telecom away.

I'm Hiding Underwater with a Crew of Naked Elves

The nurse caught me dissociating while I was driving. I was on my way to the supermarket to pick up a couple of boxes of masala tea when she ambushed me. Pulling a machete out of her bosom, she threatened me with imprisonment so everyone jumped in the lake. Bare bellies hit the sound barrier like a smattering of applause but I arrived just short of the punchline.

I moved estates, changed my name and never looked back. Began spying on the neighbours through a crack in the conservatory and wrote a script based on true events. Developed a fear of cleaning ovens or filing for divorce. Employed a Christian lawyer, on the grounds of being sanctimonious. Picked olives instead of grapes and wiggled a bit every time I saw myself on screen.

Familial Links

My granny and I have matching tattoos. Big skulls that span our shoulder-blades. We got them done together, arrived at the parlour rough and naked like plucked turkeys. We stuck like slugs to the plastic benches, revelling in the discomfort we gave the artist with our wobbling, iridescent flesh. He crawled out from behind his desk, gun poised in defence.

When the needle pierced my skin I felt sexy like a porn star or a kid wearing sparkly plastic heels. He wouldn't look at either of us while he worked but I have my granny's eyes and I told her it looked fine. The ink ticked like a pipe cleaner and for days after I danced against door frames to try and make sense of it all.

I Hate You

You hurt me enough to
swallow the sea whole
and regurgitate it back up
over a Sunday roast
feel the salt burn my throat
clamp my sharp teeth
on your wrist and lock my jaw
an increased pressure
buildup that renders you
limp and squealing.

Fame and Glory

I got too much sleep last night,
and now I'm in a Wes Anderson film
and he's telling me to tie my shoelaces properly.
Slow zoom on an olive bowl.
I can see stretched faces on the glistening fronts
but the trick shots are over here.
It's purely business, playing scrabble
with a serial killer is a minimum-wage
transaction in his communist state.
Cut to the emblematic disco ball.
Have you forgotten your lines?
There's a statistic from 1982
that says I'll never get married
unless violets are involved. I suppose
that's up to the costume department.
Wes starts shouting,
apparently we're too melancholy.
Walking absences of joy that were
predisposed to depression the moment
we picked up our pencils.
I wouldn't expect to feel anything else.

Scorpion

Shoot me between the toes then
serenade me silly.
Scream at me until you're raw.
Seduce me in the moonlight.
Sellotape a bank
statement to my car.
Sing to me
shirtless,
sunbathe in my
skin and I'll immortalise you in
scripture. Talk to me
sunny and
straddle me in
spider shoes.
Soothe my melodrama. Tell me it
stings and I'll
strangle you anyway.

Father Figure

The common ground between art and science;
a walking dichotomy of afflictions.
"Pick your poison"
wrinkly white matter
but it's different shades of teal.
Analytical number crunch
with a caffeine twitch to the untrained eye.
Deft with figures, useless with cheques
and a union for crosshatches and stencils cut at razor point.

Retractable blades and cataphysical space,
there's a perverse punctuality to
the status quo that doesn't sit quite right
with a polymath of the current age.
Modern-day testing in a souped-up drugstore
makeup brand of the same vein,
his prescriptivist impulses at odds with the nib and pen.

Sundays at 53

Every single one was sunlight and dust, cherries on the kitchen table and coffee smoke close behind. Dark red ceilings, mahogany furniture and dried patina in the cracks between scenes.

During summer the parquet floors breathe back and we stick to the leather sofa, staring sweaty faces through television screens. In winter the corners feel more significant; stark yellows and fissure reparations. Rooms become rich and take on the colour and smell of spiced salami.

Self-awareness is the singular requirement, to paint and write and absorb sunshine from crinkled sheets. I remember tracing carpeted geometrics and learning strings of numbers for the fun of it.

Dancing through strung sheets and trapping afternoons in-between mirrors, we indulged in crystallised sugar and sweet rind cubes beneath a glass angel playing the flute.

There's metallic wallpaper and a room full of rubbish. A temporary art studio, a net curtain, a harp amongst cloth. Guests love the warmth; it's rich and interesting and eclectic and disorganised.

A tangy smell and two cans of Febreze over a dust sheet. Ice lolly stick in a puddle of syrup. 8 kids on bouncy hoppers and a ball-pit for the parents. Families line up under a lens like shrimps in a bell jar.

Response to Simryn Gill's 'Channel #12'

I was shot torn and raggedy,
strung up on a branch like a warning sign.
Last Wednesday I choked on a loose tooth
and never even saw it coming.
We're retching on grit and clumps
of hair are clogging the sewers.
There's a trampoline stuck in my drainpipe
and it's starting to smell like a soup kitchen.
I like my steak griddled medium-low,
you're chewing on tendons and soon they're going to snap.
Gristle nestled in your gums,
can you hear that tapping on the back of your neck?
It's party hour and the candles are on their lowest setting.
It doesn't matter how much power we save
when there's polyester everywhere!
We're decorating beaches like
Christmas trees,
navigating gondolas through plastic bags,
caramel-coated and scrunched up like daisies.
Whoops mind the gap!
I'm fishing for life in a plughole and the residue stings.
A dead seal slid across the kitchen floor.
Too bad he never introduced himself,
I'm a big one for salutations.

Reality

Your fingernails are made of glass
and when you bite them, shards
pierce your gums; making them bleed.
Your sister is a firework - tugged at the ends
by each parent. On
your uncle's 42nd birthday she explodes
with the noise of an overweight man
eating a bag of crisps
and everything smells like gasoline.
Today you promised yourself that
last Tuesday you'll learn to love
your seven toes,
and that it doesn't matter that the
furniture doesn't like you,
or that everyone calls you "Alstroemeria"
despite your name being "Moon".
At night your teddy bears kiss each other
and during the day your mother's hands
turn into electric whisks. We're all
suspended at the violet end of a rainbow,
and the pot of gold got stuck in the
chimney. Last week your grandmother
gave you a locket; inside was a
dead unicorn. You've tried, but you just
can't get its sparkly blood off your carpet.

On Second Thought

You know that type of silence
when you can feel somebody there?
It's static, the space between heart contractions.
Tense, momentary and fleeting.
The feeling before pain. You've jumped
off the bridge but you're not wet either.

She heard the sound before she saw his lips move.
Recoil of a shotgun,
barrel down the back,
damp pressing on the tongue. It's defence
without accusation, hallucinations in the headlights.
She's started dancing but there's no music.

Finger on the pulse - he's alive but only slowly.
They blame it on pills, hot water, air compression -
that sort of thing.
Paint peels, cracks inch towards the frame.
The murderer falls before he's killed.
The victim says he saw God

because that's what you're supposed to say,
but really he smelt the magnification
of oil in a fat fryer fishbowl.
The distribution of weight can feel like an apology.
Anticipation sure feels heavy;
socks meet carpet like reunited lovers.

Writer's Manifesto

At twelve I came home from school with a drawing of an ape. My mum spilt her tea and suddenly the ape looked a little watery. Six years later I came home with a shit tattoo and I was the one crying. They say that apes are as intelligent as humans but lack the ability to express it. My whole life has been an expression of feelings. I have a lot of dreams, most of which are sad. Last night I imagined embracing a shiny-eyed stranger and woke up sobbing.

Anxiety is my catalyst for creativity and I haven't felt this uneasy in a while. Imagine if every time you felt like flying you actually did. I like the word 'limn', it's defined as 'to depict or describe in painting or words'. My favourite people are a subset of these terms. To be understood, a poem needs to be read once. To dissect is to kill. People don't want to read what you think they want to read.

Duane Michals' 'Real Dreams' helped me with this. He is an orange and the other photographers are apples. I like the reference to fruit, I am a berry. Schools teach that creativity is a luxury to the curriculum but it's a chore; you have to push it. Colours and words are the foundations of everything you've ever known. All writers are liars; the truth is malleable. My favourite poem is the one where they hide from a shooter in a supermarket.

Thinking about the future makes me twitch but I hope for the best. Protests are a more permeable alternative to Twitter. We're all given too much voice and suddenly everyone's a motivator. Pain is a social construct and its time the architect of this house paid attention to the mortar. Most people strive for money but I just pray I articulate everything I need to. Tell the saints we're all looking at the next best thing and dear God I hope we make it.

Past Love

Picture a sewer rat hanging from a leather thread, Blu Tack caught in its scraggly fur. Spittle dried in the crevice of your mouth, you ate my spaghetti and it all went downhill from there. Blowing bubbles on the freeway, we're floating down the steam but there's a parked ambulance beneath. I screamed at you to catch my breath but the postman doesn't deliver on Sundays.

We spent the summer in Scunthorpe getting sunburnt on a metal slide. Soft violet like a bubonic farmland, this drum only beats for the lucky few. Tactility springs softly under the gaze of a frenchman's bulldog, but we see no reason to care. Strip search the do-gooder who eats ibuprofen for breakfast. It's a Fanta bruise in the back of a Vista Cruiser and you just can't keep your feet still.

My mojo came back to me in an email after I saw Slipknot live and the audience had finished crying. You meant more to me than a packet of cigs, left brow sweating above its counterpart and I struggled to contain my laughter. Our fingernails liked each other's company more than the next yet we couldn't seem to spend enough money.

Kids in America

There are no left hand shakes or kick flips, it's all $1 pizza and knuckles and wet tongues. Polar bears don't need ice caps, they need metropolitan connections and liberal healthcare but the leaders say "NO!" Don't scream, it alarms your neighbours but you wouldn't know anything about that because you were born on a live stream pipe dream.

Teenagers are big and scary - they'll eat your teeth for an afternoon snack, but do you know what's meaner? Big jaws on the rind of a dried salmon, two left feet on the back of the wheel and an incarcerated soldier sunny-side up. "Who's the head of state around here?" Are we talking about liquidations or carbonations? These things aren't real - why don't you fornicate on the treasureland? We're in a constant state of arousal but the villagers don't deem it appropriate.

Suck it up hunnybun. We're told to hit the ground running, young gun in the back of our tongues. Deep sea diver on a shore-length cliff, you handed your resignation slip to the mayor but he wouldn't authorise your demise. Please, SOMEBODY do something!! Tables are turning faster than you can yell "MOVE" and that's on the pizza party arriving late. Take us to your leader and we'll spit in his face. The budgie's finished singing, now it's time to riot.

End of the Line

Blood is thicker than water, until there's blood in the water and the sheets are stained. It's easy to remove blood with water as long as the blood is warm and the water is not. If blood is hereditary then where are my blue eyes and lobeless ears? Why did my sister get Grandad's kindness but I got his spleen? There's too much tissue in a pre-cut bandage, the war hero knows best. Think about all the bloodlines you could've retrieved if you hadn't been preoccupied with your own. Nobody owns me so why does my reputation feel like a commodity? Forget the silver spoon, I came from fighters and writers and victims of arson in broad daylight. It's an interdisciplinary Venn diagram and the ancestral demands are heavier than you'd think. Alveoli branch of the respiratory system, diamond dog collar on a trust-fund prodigy.

Community Service

Day one at the care home. Plastic blue socks have been attached to underside of shoes for approximately fourteen minutes and fifty two seconds before one of them croaks it. Cue the medical nurse with a body bag while I rattle a tin of custard creams to distract a room of unbothered crones.

Phase two: everyone witnesses the death rattle, deaf cat included. Marjorie makes a bad joke about a cup of tea aaaand there goes Harold. Someone get the team, we're gonna need another bag. Call me silly but I wasn't aware that corpses routinely relieve themselves. Two mops and a retractable blade later, there's a naked body on a wheeled trolley and a piss-soaked settee on the front drive.

It's finally 3pm, and this week's activity is discotheque. Out come the battery-operated lights and an iridescent pom pom from 1937. Begin the cheesy hits playlist while everyone slumps as glum as before. The volume is cranked a couple of notches but I doubt it's reached their frequency range. Thirty five minutes of forced dancing and I'm out of there faster than the average casket.

Taking Accountability For Things

I lost God in a multi-storey complex.

I was too busy snaffling a micro pig to take any notes.

I froze my fallopian tubes for a mediocre pay out.

Buy my merch and I'll never go away.

Sweet dreams are made of polystyrene and vitamins.

Sorry I'm not a philanthropist.

I thought it read 'Do Not Resuscitate'.

I'm addicted to beer.

There's a parachute in my mouth.

It's a birth defect.

I forgot how to use the microwave.

Punk Rock died years ago.

I'm only fifteen.

I'm a part-time compartmentaliser.

I was stabbed in my sleep.

I'm powerless in the scheme of things but here's ink and a potato.

It doesn't come with a spoon.

We've run out of soap.

It's not my fault I'm allergic.

Ant Farm

I've started dreaming about events before we knew there was a problem with the lake, back when we argued about how your ant farm took up too much space in the shed and I said it was cruel and you said it was life so I would sneak out and feed them strawberry seeds when you weren't looking. I liked to think the ants were having a pretty good time before the afternoon when the pipes burst and the shed flooded and we scrambled to save them but we didn't reach the little glass box in time and it floated away, bobbing casually like sweethearts on a foreign exchange and we filed a missing colony report two hours later but nobody took us seriously because who even keeps ants without a stable shed and a breeding permit? I remember sweating like somebody's uncle and finding a cardboard box to try and replace them until you pointed out it was useless, that no two ants are the same and I'm pretty sure that moment gave birth to the rest of our lives. In the dreams my voice bounces across the lake and I'm wading to the centre but something's off and when I look down I'm not wet at all I'm trapped in a glass cage and I'm sinking in the lake with nobody except ants to blame and that's when my palms begin to itch and I wake with the feeling of chaos that started that day and have never been able to shake.

Butterfly Effect

The self-prophetic tennis player misses all her serves, and the introspective dinner lady forgets her keys, and the reliable drunk wakes up south side of his kitchen table, and the ageing gardener loses chopsticks in her teeth, and the evaluative estate agent installs spyware on his girlfriend's phone and the supermarket manager eats pudding for breakfast, and the landscape architect forgets to design a junction, so as a consequence somewhere in East Anglia someone is late for his interview and misses an encounter with what would have been the love of his life by seconds, and the cleaner who mopped the floors that day plugs an android named Annabel into her kitchen conservatory, signalling an electrical overload that causes a fuse blow and all the antiquated houses on her estate in the west district of central Derbyshire miss the England game, and simultaneously stomp the floor yelling "Shiiiit", whilst in a small town in Nigeria a mother coughs up triplets.

Clean Slate

I'm as raw as the day I was born.
Pink-bellied and screaming,
I'm surprised nobody offered
an accompanying bass lift.
I'm spaced in Cyprus while my body
spends the day in Manchester.
She's gone to get her tattoo removed,
I hope she's having fun. Surgery on her heel
but the train's late and she's rubbing skin
on the sidelines to get herself home.
There's a story about a man
who was involved in an accident.
He burnt his entire body except his left foot,
and so to avoid the pain he became his foot.
Constructed an entire narrative
through the perspective of a trodden appendage.
Mine looks like Jesus,
like a puncture wound,
like the golden archetype of Achilles,
pinched at the sleeves and dipped in butter.
A misprint, photocopy error.
There are two tattoos for the price of one,
etched on a pair of strangers.
One's unbothered and the other's
frantically scrubbing with the blue end of an eraser.

THINGS TO DO

straw jam
d's gum
unsalted butter
me gum
ham (breaded)

Incarceration

Janine's life is collapsing in a small-scale vacuum.
It's an abridged affair, a succinct selection of sorts.
She's got liver scars and a hummingbird heart
and the doctor's won't let her breathe. Locked in
a stubborn cell in Lancashire, her pillow blinks
back at her and the password to access her bathroom
is 'SPREADJESUSNOTGERMS'. The weekly
strip-searches are the most affection she gets and
even the priest avoids her at confession time.
Every day she whispers to the institution's cat
and it cries "pa zzzzing" right back.

'If I could wake up in a different place,
at a different time,
could I wake up as a different person?'

- Chuck Palahniuk

Author's Biography

Sophie Norton is a 20 year old writer and university student, currently completing a degree in English Literature.

She was commended in the 2018 Foyle Young Poets award with her sestina 'Cactus', and has since had her poems published in various anthologies including 'The Rabbit Hole', 'Viral Verses', and 'My Brain In All Its Perfidious Beauty', as well as in the independent American Magazines 'Rambler!' and 'Unpublished'.

She is a journalist for London-based 'Lightwork Magazine', and is head of the Blog team for the student-run Norman Rea Gallery in York.

Printed in Great Britain
by Amazon